CAN SCIENCE SOLVE ?

THE MYSTERY OF THE
BERMUDA TRIANGLE

Chris Oxlade

Heinemann Library
Chicago, Illinois

Customer Service 888-454-2279
Visit our website at www.heinemannraintree.com

Designed by Victoria Bevan and Q2A
Printed and bound in China by WKT

10 09 08 07 06
10 9 8 7 6 5 4 3 2 1

New edition ISBNs: 1-40348-336-1 (hardcover)
                   1-40348-345-0 (paperback)

The Library of Congress has cataloged the hardcover editions as follows:
Oxlade, Chris.
        The mystery of the Bermuda Triangle / Chris Oxlade.
p. cm. - (Can science solve?)
Includes bibliographical references and index.
Summary: Discusses the Bermuda Triangle, an area of the Atlantic Ocean where numerous ships and airplanes have mysteriously disappeared, and examines various efforts to identify this phenomena and discover its causes.
        ISBN 1-57572-811-7 (lib. bdg.)
Bermuda Triangle Juvenile literature [1. Bermuda triangle.]
I.   Title. II. Series
G558.095   1999
001.94.—dc21
                                                              99-18042
                                                              CIP

Acknowledgments
The author and publishers are grateful to the following for permission to reproduce copyright material:
Austin J. Brown: pp. 11, 13, 15; James David Travel Photography: p. 28; Mary Evans Picture Library: pp. 5, 6, 9; Eye Ubiquitous: p. 16, S Lindridge p. 22; FLPA: D Fleetham/Silvestris p. 7 (inset), H Hoflinger p. 17, D Kinzler p. 18; Fortean Picture Library: pp. 24, 27, W Donato p. 21; National Archives: pp. 8, 10; The People: p. 29; Trip: E Smith p. 7 (main).

Cover photograph of a storm at sea, reproduced with permission of Getty/Taxi.

Every effort has been made to contact copyright holders of any material reproduced in this book. Any omissions will be rectified in subsequent printings if notice is given to the publisher.

The paper used to print this book comes from sustainable sources.

Some words are shown in bold, **like this**. You can find the definitions for these words in the glossary.

CONTENTS

UNSOLVED MYSTERIES

For hundreds of years, people have been interested in and puzzled by mysterious places, creatures, and events. What secrets does a **black hole** hold? Are some houses really haunted by ghosts? Does the Abominable Snowman actually exist? Why do ships and planes vanish without a trace when they cross the Bermuda Triangle? These mysteries have baffled scientists, who have spent years trying to find the answers. But just how far can science go? Can it really explain the seemingly unexplainable? Or are there some mysteries that science simply cannot solve? Read on, and make up your own mind . . .

This book tells you about the Bermuda Triangle. It looks in detail at some of the unexplained disappearances that have happened in it, retells accounts from eyewitnesses, and investigates whether science can account for some of these bizarre events.

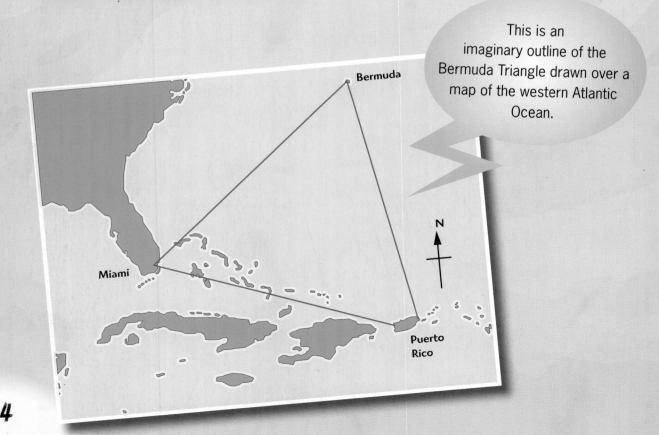

This is an imaginary outline of the Bermuda Triangle drawn over a map of the western Atlantic Ocean.

Bermuda

Miami

Puerto Rico

N

Bermuda Triangle briefing

Bermuda is made up of about 150 small islands, 620 miles (1,000 kilometers) out into the Atlantic Ocean from the eastern coast of the United States. The area known as the Bermuda Triangle is, not surprisingly, a triangle with its three points in Bermuda, in Miami, Florida, and in Puerto Rico (see map). The term *Bermuda Triangle* was first used by U.S. journalist Vincent Gaddis in 1964 when he wrote a magazine article with the title "The Deadly Bermuda Triangle," in which he listed mysterious disappearances in the area.

Over the last 200 years, thousands of boats, ships, and aircraft have run into trouble in the Bermuda Triangle. Most of these cases have a perfectly reasonable explanation, but almost 100 of them remain a mystery. Could they be caused by some strange, unknown force? Is there anything science can do to solve the mystery?

Is it a triangle?

Many writers do not agree about the boundaries of the Bermuda Triangle. A few say that it is a triangle, while others that it is an elongated, four-sided shape called the Devil's Triangle or the Limbo of the Lost, which stretches farther into the Atlantic.

JUNE

25 CENTS
IN CANADA 30 CENTS

AMAZING STORIES

Scientifiction
Stories by
A. Hyatt Verrill
John W. Campbell, Jr.
Edmond Hamilton

Disappearances in the Bermuda Triangle gave rise to many wild and wonderful stories in science-fiction magazines.

BEGINNINGS OF A MYSTERY

Although it was not until the 1960s that the Bermuda Triangle became famous, it had been an area of mystery for sailors long before then. It all started when early voyagers, including Christopher Columbus, who first sailed through the Bermuda Triangle area in 1492, encountered unfamiliar sights and strange goings-on.

Christopher Columbus sailed through the Triangle in the *Santa Maria*, a small ship called a caravel.

A sea of weed

One of these strange sights was the area now known as the Sargasso Sea, an oval-shaped patch of the North Atlantic Ocean several hundred miles across, stretching well into the Bermuda Triangle. In the Sargasso Sea, the water is normally calm, with little wind and **current**, and the water is also more salty than the surrounding sea, with very little **plankton** and very few fish. Strangest of all, there are huge rafts of seaweed called Sargassum weed. Seaweed is hardly ever found in the open ocean.

To the early sailors, the seaweed suggested that they were near land, so they were confused when no land appeared. The weed also became tangled with their ships, slowing them down, and the light winds often left them drifting for days on end. It's no wonder, then, that tales spread of ships trapped forever or pulled under the sea by the weeds, and of sailors eaten by hideous sea creatures.

Columbus also reported seeing strange lights in the sky in the area and said his ships' compasses behaved strangely. When he returned with a fleet of ships 10 years after his first trip, he had lost 12 in a fierce hurricane. The island of Bermuda itself was not settled until about 100 years after this, mainly because it had a reputation as a "place for devils."

There is no doubt that hundreds of ships were lost in the Bermuda Triangle over the following centuries. Many sank without a trace and were assumed to have been overwhelmed by storms. The first ship that is mentioned in the literature on the Bermuda Triangle is the U.S. warship USS *Pickering*, which disappeared without a trace in 1800.

SHIPS AND BOATS

Losses of ships and boats in the Bermuda Triangle fall into two groups: those where the ship or boat disappeared without a trace and those where the ship or boat was found, but with the crew missing.

Spray

(**Sloop**, vanished in 1909)

The *Spray* was sailed by Joshua Slocum, an experienced sailor who was the first man to sail alone around the world. It disappeared with Slocum, who was 65 years old at the time, after he had visited Miami for supplies.

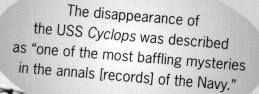

The disappearance of the USS *Cyclops* was described as "one of the most baffling mysteries in the annals [records] of the Navy."

Cyclops

(U.S. Navy **collier**, vanished in 1918)

The *Cyclops*, 540 feet (165 meters) long, weighing 19,300 tons (17,500 tonnes), and with 300 crew, is one of the largest ships lost in the Triangle. It disappeared without a trace on its way from the island of Barbados to the eastern United States. The *Cyclops* was the first ship to disappear that carried a radio, but the crew sent no emergency message.

Carroll A Deering

(Five-masted **schooner**, found abandoned in 1921)

The *Carroll A Deering* left Rio de Janeiro, in Brazil, without cargo to return to Norfolk, Virginia. Several weeks later, it was seen by the crew of a **lightship**, under full sail with the crew all together on the deck. One of the crew shouted that they had lost both anchors. Two days later, the ship was found beached on the shore with the sails still set and the lifeboats and crew's belongings on board. However, the crew themselves were missing and never seen again.

Marine Sulfur Queen

(Cargo ship, vanished in 1963)

The *Marine Sulfur Queen* left Texas carrying a cargo of molten (melted) sulfur. A search was started when it could not be contacted after failing to send a routine radio message. Some debris (wreckage), including a foghorn and life jacket, was found.

The Mary Celeste

Easily the most famous mystery of the sea is the case of the *Mary Celeste*, a small sail-powered cargo ship that was found drifting without its crew in 1872. The case of the *Mary Celeste* is often linked with the Bermuda Triangle, but it was actually found near the Azores, which are closer to Spain than the United States. According to many accounts of the case, the ship appeared as normal, with all the crew's possessions and all the cargo on board. It seemed that the crew had magically vanished. However, there was some damage to the rigging (ropes and chains), the lifeboat was missing, and the hold (interior) was full of seawater. The most likely explanation of the many put forward is that the crew was convinced that the ship was about to sink and abandoned it in a hurry without taking down the sails. The ship continued to sail, leaving them behind in mid-ocean in an overloaded lifeboat.

INTO THIN AIR

Nothing, not a scrap of aircraft or any survivors, has ever been found in any of the cases of aircraft that have disappeared in the Bermuda Triangle.

Flight 19

(Five U.S. Navy bombers and a rescue plane, vanished in 1945)

The case of Flight 19 is the most famous of all aircraft cases. It is mysterious because a group of five aircraft vanished at the same time along with the search plane that was sent to find them—all of which seems a very unlikely combination of events. There are many different accounts of this case, but here are the basic facts.

At 2 P.M. on December 5, five Avenger torpedo bombers took off in good weather from Fort Lauderdale, Florida, on a routine training mission that should have lasted two hours. The first signs of trouble appeared at 3:45 P.M., when the pilots realized they were lost. The flight leader, Lieutenant Taylor, reported that both his compasses were "out." A flight instructor from Fort Lauderdale offered to fly south to meet them, but Taylor replied, "I know where I am now. Don't come after me."

This is a Martin Mariner seaplane, similar to the one that was sent to search for Flight 19.

Messages between the planes were heard at about 7 P.M., and a Martin Mariner seaplane was sent to search for them at 7:30 P.M. Nothing more was heard from any of the Avengers or the Mariner, and an extensive air-sea rescue search found no sign of the 27 airmen.

Star Tiger

(Tudor IV airliner, vanished in 1948)

After flying from the Azores islands, the British airliner *Star Tiger* had nearly reached Bermuda when the pilot radioed that the weather was good and that he expected to arrive on time. However, the aircraft never arrived, and a search for survivors and wreckage revealed nothing.

Douglas DC-3

(Airliner, vanished in 1948)

This aircraft was flying to Miami, Florida, from Puerto Rico. The pilot reported by radio that he was 50 miles (80 kilometers) south of the airfield, but soon after this the airfield could not get a response from the DC-3. A search found no sign of the aircraft, even though the water in the area where it disappeared was only 19.6 feet (6 meters) deep. The DC-3 had simply vanished.

This is an Avro Tudor airliner similar to the one that disappeared over the Triangle in 1948.

DID YOU SEE THAT?

Many people have had strange experiences as they traveled through the Bermuda Triangle, but lived to tell the tale. Here are the stories of a few of them.

Crew of Boeing 707

Soon after takeoff from San Juan, Puerto Rico, in 1963, the crew of a 707 saw the sea below them froth up for about 30 seconds. The disturbed area was about 0.6 mile (1 kilometer) across and the froth reached several hundred feet into the air.

Chuck Wakely

In 1964 Chuck Wakely was flying from Nassau, in the Bahamas, to Miami, Florida. He noticed a faint glow on the wings, which gradually increased to a blinding light. At the same time, the aircraft's electrical equipment began to have problems. After five minutes, the glow gradually faded and things returned to normal.

Captain Don Henry

Don Henry was the captain of a **salvage tug**. In 1966 it was towing a barge (a large, flat-bottomed boat used for cargo) when it experienced electrical and engine failures and the compass started spinning out of control. Henry went out on deck to find the horizon covered by fog, the sea choppy, and the barge invisible, even though the tow rope was still tight. After a while, the engines began working again and the tug moved forward. As it did, the barge reappeared and was found to be warm to the touch.

Bruce Gernon

In 1970 Bruce Gernon was flying a small, private aircraft through the Bermuda Triangle when he flew into a "big, doughnut-shaped cloud." His instruments and compass failed and his plane felt weightless for a few seconds. When he landed, Gernon realized that he had flown 12 miles (19.3 kilometers) in twenty seconds. This should have taken three minutes. In 2005 Gernon published a book about his experience, called *The Fog*.

Crew of the USS Richard E. Byrd

In 1971 this naval destroyer lost the use of all its communications equipment on the way to Bermuda. The ship was lost and helpless at sea for more than a week before its radio began to work again.

Crew of the Hollyhock

In 1974 the **radar** aboard the *Hollyhock*, a U.S. Coast Guard boat, detected a large land mass, like an island, in the ocean. The radar was checked, but seemed to be working properly. Other ships also reported the same event. As the boat traveled toward it, the object disappeared.

Many of the stories of strange happenings in the Bermuda Triangle involve **navigational** instruments. Could this be the key to solving the mystery?

THE THEORIES

What are the possible explanations for the strange cases listed on the previous pages? A look at the reasons for marine and air accidents all over the world shows that there is a wide range of possible reasons for every disappearance in the Bermuda Triangle.

The first thing to note is that if you compare the number of accidents and disappearances in the Bermuda Triangle to the number of ships and aircraft passing through it, the Bermuda Triangle does not seem to be a particularly dangerous place. In fact, Lloyd's, the world's major **insurance** company for shipping, says that there are no more losses than in any other shipping area.

A simple explanation

Most losses at sea and in the air are not in the slightest bit mysterious—and that includes losses in the Bermuda Triangle. Losses can be caused by mechanical failure, bad weather, human error, or a combination of the three.

There are several ways a ship can be sunk. Its hull can develop a hole by hitting an object in or under the water, which allows water in from underneath; it can be damaged in a collision; it can simply break apart; or it can **capsize** because it is top-heavy, overloaded, or its cargo moves to one side. Obviously, bad weather makes all these events more likely. In the case of a collision, a smaller craft can be hit and sunk by a much larger craft without the crew of the larger craft even noticing, especially at night.

In an aircraft, a **structural failure**, such as the loss of a wing, or a control failure, such as the **rudder** jamming, can bring it down very quickly. In both ships and aircraft, there can also be fires or explosions because of dangerous cargo or leaking fuel tanks.

Human factors

Mistakes by ships' crews and aircraft pilots can cause accidents. At sea, where there are no landmarks, **navigational** errors can lead to ships and aircraft without modern navigational equipment becoming hopelessly lost. This is almost certainly what happened to the ill-fated Flight 19—the aircraft probably ran out of fuel and crashed into the ocean. Bad design or poor maintenance can also be responsible for mechanical failures. A few ships also disappear without a trace because of insurance fraud, **sabotage**, and the actions of modern-day pirates.

This shows an old DC-3 airliner on landing approach. In the 1940s, aircraft did not have the advanced navigation equipment that today's aircraft do.

STRANGE WEATHER

The seas in the Bermuda Triangle are often featured in vacation brochures, where they look calm, turquoise, and shallow. But in fact, the area is prone to very bad storms, from gusty thunderstorms to **tornadoes** and **hurricanes**. The storms are often more sudden and violent than anywhere else in the world. So, does the weather hold the answer to some of the mysterious disappearances?

Hurricanes and storms

Hurricanes are enormous, swirling weather systems that are born in the Atlantic near the equator and sweep north, normally into the Caribbean Sea and the Gulf of Mexico. In the center of a hurricane, winds can reach average speeds of more than 93 miles (150 kilometers) per hour, gusting to 186 miles (300 kilometers) per hour.

Thunderstorms are created when warm, damp air rises and **condenses**. They can be huge and severe in the Bermuda Triangle, with clouds reaching up to 49,200 feet (15,000 meters) high and measuring several miles across. Under the clouds are strong, gusty winds and sometimes small, hurricane-like mini storms.

This is a hurricane photographed from space. The strongest winds are near the center of the swirl of cloud.

These super-strong hurricane and storm winds and the huge waves they create can overwhelm and **capsize** small boats, cause ships to break apart, and blow ships off course. Inside the storm clouds themselves, the winds are very turbulent—they blow up and down as well as sideways. Aircraft flying through them are tossed around, occasionally so fiercely that their structure is damaged.

Freak waves

Even large ships have been capsized by individual freak waves, which can be up to 115 feet (35 meters) high. They may be caused by undersea earthquakes or volcanic eruptions, landslides on the **continental shelf**, or by storm waves building together.

A waterspout is a tornado that sucks up water from the sea, destroying any small craft in its way.

Currents

The water in the Bermuda Triangle also has strong **currents** flowing in it. These include the strong, north-flowing current called the Gulf Stream, which flows at about 4.3 miles (7 kilometers) per hour. Wind blowing in the opposite direction to the current can create very high waves that can flood and capsize small craft. These currents could explain many of the unsuccessful air-sea searches in the Bermuda Triangle, because by the time the rescue services arrive at the scene of the accident, the wreckage would have been swept away and spread apart.

ELECTRICITY AND MAGNETISM

Many travelers in the Bermuda Triangle experience strange magnetic and electrical effects, such as spinning compasses, failed electrical equipment, drained batteries, radio interference, and peculiar lights. Are there any natural phenomena that could explain these effects?

Lightning happens when static electricity that builds up inside a cloud jumps to the ground.

Lightning

The heat created by a lightning strike can cause explosions on ships and in aircraft if the sparks set fire to fuel or fuel vapor (liquid fuel turned to gas) inside empty fuel tanks. It can sink wooden ships by punching holes in the **hull**. The huge **electric currents** in lightning also create strong **magnetic fields** that can make compasses swing and interfere with radio communications.

Ball lightning

Ball lightning is very rare and not fully understood by scientists, but it could explain some of the strange lights seen in the Triangle. It comes in the form of a ball of colored light, normally about 9.8 inches (25 centimeters) across, and forms in **electrical storms**. The ball can hover and move around, as if under remote control.

Strange magnetic fields

Earth acts as a giant magnet, with its **magnetic poles** near, but not in the same place as, its **geographic poles**. A magnetic compass points toward magnetic north, which is the direction toward the magnetic North Pole. In most places on Earth's surface, there is a difference between magnetic north and true north. However, the Bermuda Triangle is on a line through both the geographic North Pole and the magnetic North Pole, so the two directions are the same. A compass pointing to true north seems strange to sailors and pilots from other areas of the world, and it could explain some **navigational** errors in the Triangle.

Another confusing compass error, which happens in many areas of the world, including some parts of the Bermuda Triangle, is when the compass turns away from magnetic north. These incidents are often caused by hidden deposits of iron ore or magnetic rocks under the ground, which distort Earth's magnetic field. The effect is called a **magnetic anomaly**. Temporary magnetic anomalies could also be caused by **magma** flowing near Earth's surface, by undersea earthquakes, and by electrical storms. It is possible that these events could set up extremely strong magnetic fields, which could affect electrical equipment as well as compasses.

A piece of iron changes the shape of a magnet's field just as magnetic rocks affect Earth's magnetic field.

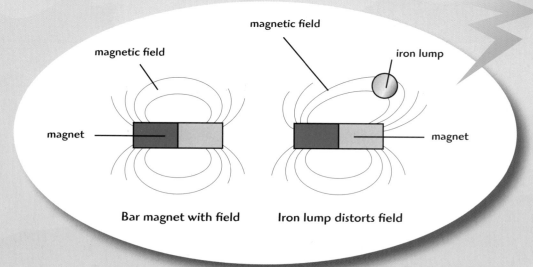

magnetic field

magnetic field

iron lump

magnet

magnet

Bar magnet with field

Iron lump distorts field

WEIRD AND WONDERFUL

Several Bermuda Triangle "experts" who have written books on the subject claim that the strange events that happen there cannot have natural explanations. How, they say, can huge ships and whole groups of aircraft simply disappear in calm weather and shallow seas? Instead, they argue that some sort of **supernatural** forces are involved. The only evidence for these theories is the lack of evidence—that the disappeared craft and people have never been found.

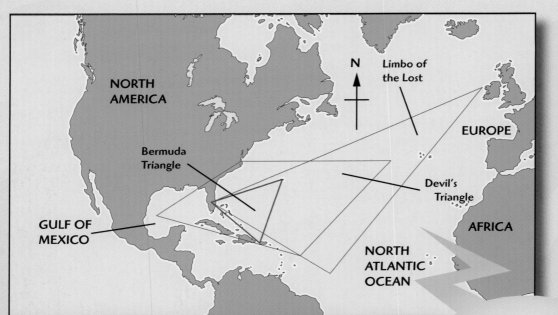

Writers question the boundaries of the Bermuda Triangle, possibly so that disappearances can be included in their arguments.

Vile vortices

Ivan T. Sanderson drew up a map of areas where strange disappearances happen, including the Bermuda Triangle and the "Devil's Sea" near Japan. He suggests that there are twelve such areas, which he calls "vile vortices," where there are huge **magnetic anomalies** that create time slips and mysteriously transport objects to other places on Earth. However, there does not seem to be any evidence to support this.

Aliens and Atlantis

One of the most popular theories for the Bermuda Triangle disappearances is that the ships and aircraft, or the people on them, have been abducted by aliens and carried away for investigation and experimentation. Ivan T. Sanderson claims that there could be an advanced civilization under the ocean below the Bermuda Triangle, and that the ships and aircraft are taken there.

The most famous Bermuda Triangle writer, Charles Berlitz, has suggested that Atlantis, the legendary lost land, was near the island of Bimini in the Bahamas, on the western edge of the Bermuda Triangle. Berlitz thinks that technology developed by the people of Atlantis is responsible for sinking ships and causing aircraft to fall into the sea. However, we only know about the legend of Atlantis from the writings of the ancient Greek philosopher Plato. There is no proof that it ever existed.

These are underwater ruins near the island of Bimini, claimed to be the remains of Atlantis.

Black holes

Vincent Gaddis, the man who coined the phrase *Bermuda Triangle* in 1964, suggested in the same article that ships and planes may be disappearing through a "gateway" (possibly a mini **black hole**) into another time or another universe. This could explain why some aircraft traveling through the Bermuda Triangle arrive at their destination more quickly than should have been possible, although **navigational** errors and unexpected strong winds are a more likely explanation.

A MODERN THEORY

In 1995 an international organization called the
Ocean Drilling Program began to investigate the ocean
floor between Bermuda and the coast of the United
States. They were looking for **methane** escaping from
the rocks under the ocean floor, which could possibly
be used as an energy source. What has this got to
do with the Bermuda Triangle? The huge bubbles of
methane escaping from the ocean bed could rise
to the surface, affecting ships and aircraft above.

Gas hydrates

The strange thing about the methane gas the drillers found was
that it was in the form of gas hydrate. This means that it was mixed
with frozen water. In methane hydrate, the methane is locked up
inside the ice. Methane hydrate is formed when a mixture of water
and methane is squeezed by very high pressure deep under the
seabed. When the pressure is released or the temperature rises,
the methane is released. When just 0.3 gallon (1 liter) of icy hydrate
melts, it releases 45 gallons (170 liters) of methane.

Scientists think that there is a huge amount of methane hydrate under
the oceans, formed as dead animals and plants decompose in the
sediments on the ocean floor. In fact, methane
hydrates have been found under the
ocean in the Bermuda Triangle.

Methane released
from the ocean floor could
explain some accidents on oil
and gas drilling rigs.

Bubble trouble

Imagine what would happen if a deposit of methane hydrate under the ocean floor were released into the water. This could happen during enormous underwater landslides or earthquakes. Remember that a small amount of hydrate makes a huge amount of gas. The bubble of gas would rush toward the surface, expanding as it did so.

If a huge bubble rose up under a ship, it would produce an enormous hole in the sea underneath it. The ship would drop into the hole and sink instantly, settle to the seabed, and be covered in sediment thrown up by the escaping gas.

The methane gas would also cause problems for aircraft above the water. Methane is lighter than air, so it would rise upward after leaving the water. An aircraft flying through the area would suffer engine failure or even ignite (set fire to) the gas. There is also evidence that a huge rush of gas would create a strong **magnetic field** that would affect compasses.

This diagram shows what could happen to a ship if a huge bubble rose underneath it.

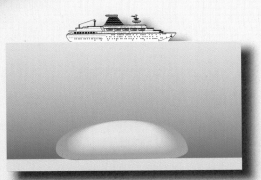

Melting gas hydrate causes methane bubble on seabed

Bubble rises to surface

Bubble causes "hole" in surface of water into which ship falls

Ship fills with water and sinks

TRUE OR FALSE?

There are no reports of disappearances being faked in the Bermuda Triangle, but there are many cases of the truth about disappearances being ignored. Most of the books about the Bermuda Triangle discuss many cases of ships and aircraft that have disappeared or been found abandoned. The problem is that the facts of the cases are misquoted, fiddled with, or simply ignored in order to make the cases seem more mysterious than they really are. Here are some of the cases. They are outlined in more detail on pages 10 and 11.

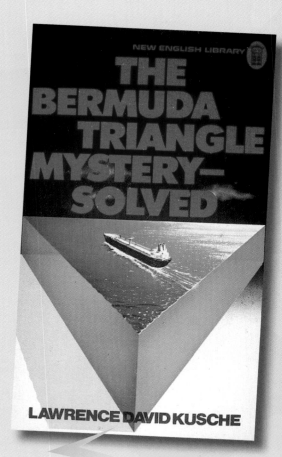

Flight 19

(Five bombers and a rescue plane, vanished in 1945)

There are reports that the flight leader sent a message saying, "This is an emergency. We seem to be off course. We cannot see land . . . repeat . . . we cannot see land," and, "We don't know which way is west. Everything is wrong . . . strange. We are not sure of any direction. The ocean doesn't look as it should." These reports are not true. The flight leader was very new to the area and it's likely that he led the flight out to sea instead of back to land. Also, the Martin Mariner rescue plane did not simply disappear. A ship at sea saw an airplane explode at the same time as it disappeared from **radar** screens. The weather **deteriorated** badly, making the search almost impossible—otherwise, wreckage may have been found.

Lawrence David Kusche investigated the facts behind dozens of Bermuda Triangle "mysteries" and found that most had a simple answer.

Star Tiger

(Airliner, vanished in 1948)

Contrary to the stories of the captain reporting good flying conditions, the weather was not good: there were strong head winds and heavy cloud cover, which made navigation difficult. The aircraft may also have run out of fuel because the strong head winds would have made the journey take longer than expected.

DC-3

(Airliner, vanished in 1948)

There are false reports that the pilot said he could "see the lights of Miami," but it is likely that he was lost and over deep ocean. The DC-3 is known to have had a faulty radio, so it could not have made an emergency call.

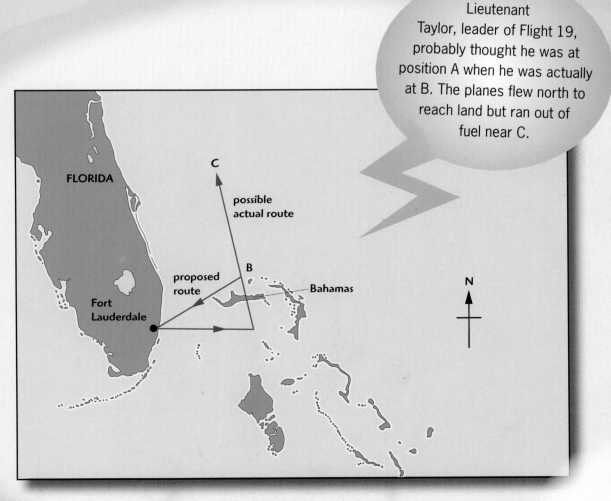

Lieutenant Taylor, leader of Flight 19, probably thought he was at position A when he was actually at B. The planes flew north to reach land but ran out of fuel near C.

FLORIDA

C

possible actual route

B

proposed route

Bahamas

Fort Lauderdale

N

MUDDLED REPORTS

Listed here are ships that, according to several writers, disappeared mysteriously in the Bermuda Triangle. Again, there is more to the stories than is often reported.

Atalanta

The *Atalanta* was a training ship that disappeared in 1880 on a voyage that included a leg through the Triangle. What reports do not mention is that nobody knows where the ship actually vanished. It also had a very inexperienced crew and would have encountered bad weather in the area it was sailing through.

Rubicon

In October 1944, this 99-ton (90-tonne) Cuban cargo ship was found drifting and abandoned off Florida with only a dog on board. The crew had mysteriously vanished. Or had they? Reports from the time say it was in port in Havana, Cuba, when the **moorings** broke in a hurricane and the ship drifted away, leaving the crew stranded ashore.

Bella

This British ship was sailing from Rio de Janeiro to Jamaica in 1854 when it vanished "without a trace." It was probably overloaded and may have **capsized**. Wreckage was found six days after it left Rio, when it would have been nowhere near the Triangle.

Freya

The German **bark** *Freya* was found with its crew gone and its masts (poles) broken after sailing from Cuba. It was supposedly a victim of the Triangle, but it had actually sailed from Mexico and was found in the Pacific Ocean, not the Atlantic.

Raifuku Maru

This Japanese freighter vanished in the Triangle in 1925 after sending the alarming radio message, "Danger like dagger now. Come quick!" This message may be made up, since there was radio interference, and the passenger liner *Homeric* actually saw the freighter sink with all the crew aboard in "huge waves."

Why make up stories?

People are more interested in the mysterious than the ordinary, and books about the mysterious are often best-sellers. This is certainly true of the Bermuda Triangle mystery. Several writers have written books on the subject, which build up the mystery by telling only half the story.

Most famous of Bermuda Triangle authors is Charles Berlitz, who wrote two books in the 1970s. The first, *The Bermuda Triangle*, sold 20 million copies in 30 languages and made Berlitz a rich man. It led to television programs, newspaper articles, and more books, all based on something that may not be a mystery at all.

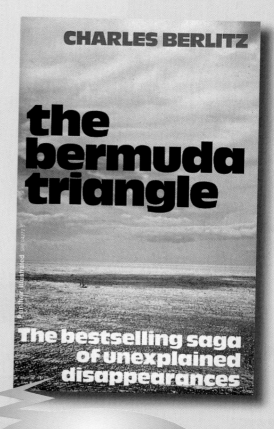

CHARLES BERLITZ

the bermuda triangle

The bestselling saga of unexplained disappearances

This is the cover of Charles Berlitz's book of "unexplained" mysteries.

WHAT DO YOU THINK?

Of all the world's mysteries, that of the Bermuda Triangle seems to be the one supported by the weakest evidence. There is no doubt that there are a few truly mysterious cases. But many of the disappearances have believable, natural explanations.

Can electricity and magnetism give us the answer?

Sounds convincing . . .

• Many travelers in the Bermuda Triangle have experienced strange magnetic effects such as spinning compasses and radio interference.

• Violent storms are common and lightning can cause fuel to explode in boats and planes.

• In some cases, unusual lights have been reported, which could be generated by electrical storms.

But what about . . . ?

• Is there any reason why these things should happen more often in the Bermuda Triangle?

• Some disappearances happened in calm weather. Can electricity and magnetism explain these?

Some people claim **supernatural** explan ations. They ignore scientific evidence of violent storms and **magnetic anomalies.** Others, including scientists, claim there is no mystery at all. They say the disappearances have natural causes and are no more frequent than probability would suggest.

What about the other theories? Do you think any of them might be true? Look at the list of theories below and think about the pros and cons of each. Decide which you think are the most convincing.

- Ships and planes in the area are abducted by aliens.

- Enormous magnetic anomalies create time slips that account for the disappearances.

- Ships and planes are sucked through a gateway similar to a **black hole**.

- Huge bubbles of **methane** hydrate rising to the surface of the ocean are responsible.

- All the disappearances in the Bermuda Triangle can be traced to bad weather or human error.

What are your conclusions? Are there theories you can dismiss without further investigation? Do you have any theories of your own? Try to keep an open mind. Remember that science is constantly evolving and new discoveries are being made all the time. Just because something can't be proved scientifically now, doesn't mean this will always be the case.

Mysteries make good reading, as this article from the *People* newspaper in 1991 demonstrates. It simply retells Triangle stories.

Fateful flight of the Avengers

AIRMEN VANISH WITHOUT TRACE

EVER since the first seamen set sail, the vast oceans have been sources of myth and mystery.

Best documented of these was last century's riddle of the Mary Celeste, the ship which was found eerily abandoned in the Atlantic, east of the Azores.

Her sails were tattered and below deck there was chilling evidence which suggested hurried flight – yet the ship's log remained intact and its last entry, made nine days before, gave no hint of impending trouble.

The mystery remained unsolved even after a British Vice Admiralty court of inquiry, as it does today.

Far more recently, voyagers of the sea and of the air have come to fear the Bermuda Triangle, a vaguely defined area somewhere east of Bermuda.

One student of the unexplained, Ivan Sanderson, has theorised that the mysterious triangle is one of a dozen areas called "vile vortices" – another infamous vortex is the so-called Devil's Sea off the coast of Japan – where baffling forces are said to cause ships to vanish.

One of the earliest of these fateful missions in the Bermuda Triangle began on December 5, 1945, when five US Avenger torpedo bombers

roared off the runway of the Fort Lauderdale Naval Air Station Florida.

Flight Instructor Lieutenant Charles G Taylor was leading 13 crewmen of Flight 19 on a routine navigational training exercise. Their course lay over an area bounded by Bermuda, Florida and Puerto Rico – the area which is now recognised as the Bermuda Triangle.

Flight 19 began smoothly enough but at 3.40pm an unsettling message from Taylor to another plane in the squadron was picked up by Lieutenant Robert Cox who was at that moment airborne over Fort Lauderdale on another exercise.

"What is your trouble?" Cox asked Taylor.

"Both my compasses are out and I am trying to find Fort Lauderdale," Taylor replied.

For 45 minutes Cox tried to ascertain Taylor's position and to direct him to land by orienting him towards the sun. But although it was a clear day, Taylor seemed unable to find it.

Finally, Taylor's transmission faded until it stopped. Then, inexplicably, Cox's radio went dead, too, and he returned to the field at Fort Lauderdale. The ground station at Fort Everglades nearby, how-

ever, had established intermittent contact with the troubled Flight 19, confirming Cox's observations. Finally, at about 5.15pm the ground station heard a forlorn message from Flight 19:

"We'll fly west until we hit the beach or run out of gas."

The authorities at Fort Lauderdale ordered a search but the Mariner was not heard of again.

For the next five days, search planes flew more than 930 sorties over the area, but not a scrap of wreckage from either the Avengers or the Mariner was ever recovered.

Most analysts blame these and other disappearances in the area on normal hazards of the sea and air. But what happened still remains a profound mystery.

More recently, we have learned of an equally mysterious leap across space and time, which occurred within the triangle – 25 years after the flight of the Avengers, almost to the day.

There was a "strange cigar-shaped cloud," recalled Bruce Gernon Jr, which gave him the first hint that his flight on December 4, 1970, would be out of the ordinary.

Gernon had just taken off in his Beachcraft Bonanza from Andros Island in the Bahamas, bound for Palm Beach, Florida.

He remembers accelerating quickly to avoid the thick cloud, but it seemed to rise to meet him.

The plane seemed to pick up unnatural speed, and for several seconds Gernon and his father experienced weightlessness. Then the aeroplane entered a greenish-white haze – not the blue sky he had seen ahead.

Through the haze he spotted a stretch of land and, calculating his flight time, took it to be the Bimini Keys, an island east of Miami. Minutes later, Gernon recognised it as Miami beach itself.

Landing at Palm Beach, Gernon checked his clock. A trip that normally took him about 75 minutes had taken him only 45. And he had burned 12 fewer gallons of fuel than usual.

To this day, Gernon considers himself a lucky voyager in the Bermuda Triangle, having lived to tell of the inexplicable time warp.

GLOSSARY

bark type of sailing cargo ship with three masts, it was popular in the late 19th century

black hole region of space where gravity is so strong not even light can escape from it

capsize become overturned

collier medium-sized cargo ship designed to carry bulk cargoes such as coal

condense turn from gas to liquid because of cooling

continental shelf edge of a continent, where the depth of the ocean increases dramatically. It can be hundreds of miles from the continent's coastline.

current flow from one place to another

deteriorate get worse

electrical storm storm in which there is lightning and thunder

electric current flow of electrical charge from one place to another. It is normally the flow of tiny particles called electrons.

geographic pole one of the two points (the North Geographic Pole and South Geographic Pole) where the axis around which Earth revolves meets Earth's surface

insurance money paid to a person if his or her property is damaged, lost, or stolen

lightship permanently anchored ship carrying a beacon to guide other ships

magma hot, molten (melted) rock under the ground

magnetic anomaly place on Earth's surface where Earth's magnetic field is distorted

magnetic field area around a magnet where its magnetic force is felt. Earth has a magnetic field shaped as though there were a bar magnet in its center.

magnetic pole one of the two places on the surface of Earth (called the North Magnetic Pole and the South Magnetic Pole) where Earth's magnetic field is strongest

methane naturally occurring gas often found under the ground with oil. Home gas supplies are often methane.

moorings buoys or jetties where boats and ships are tied up

navigational to do with navigation, which is planning and following a route at sea or in the air

phenomenon remarkable or unexplained happening

plankton numerous microscopic (tiny) animals and plants that live in seawater and freshwater

radar device that uses radio waves to detect the position of ships, aircraft, or coastlines

rudder device at the stern (rear) of a boat, ship, or aircraft that is used to make it turn from side to side

sabotage making things go wrong on purpose

salvage tug large tug used for towing ships or oil rigs or for removing ships after accidents

schooner traditional type of sailing ship with two or more masts

sediment mud, silt, sand, or small pieces of rock that are carried along by a river before settling to the bottom, when the river slows down near the sea

sloop small sailing ship

structural failure failure of the actual structure of a ship or plane, such as a hull that breaks in two or a wing that snaps off

supernatural different from the understood rules of nature

tornado swirling mass of air that reaches down from a storm cloud to the ground, normally up to 330 feet (100 meters) across, in which there are winds of more than 185 miles (300 kilometers) per hour

vortex fast-spinning swirl of air or water

Find Out More

You can find out more about the Bermuda Triangle in books and on the Internet. Use a search engine such as www.yahooligans.com to search for information. A search for the words "Bermuda Triangle" will bring back lots of results, but it may be difficult to find the information you want. Try narrowing your search to look for some of the people and ideas mentioned in this book, such as "Flight 19" or "Bruce Gernon."

More Books to Read

Donkin, Andrew. *Bermuda Triangle*. New York: DK, 2000.

Townsend, John. *Out There? Mysterious Disappearances*. Chicago: Raintree, 2004.

INDEX